PRODUCTS OF MEXICO

SOUTH OF THE BORDER

Laura Conlon

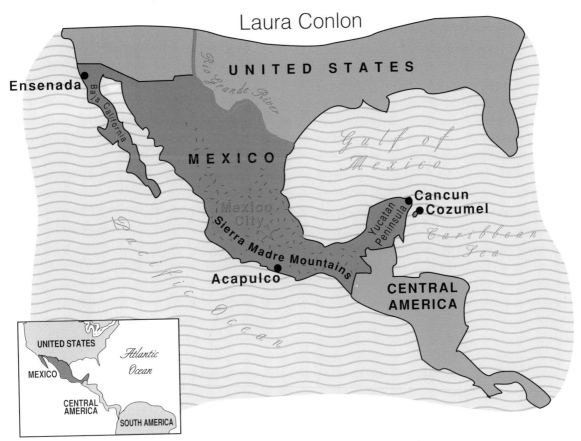

The Rourke Book Company, Inc.
Vero Beach, Florida 32964

Edited by Sandra A. Robinson

PHOTO CREDITS
© Steve Bentsen: pages 7, 15; © Francis and Donna Caldwell:
page 8; © Frank Balthis: pages 10, 17, 21; © James P. Rowan:
page 13; courtesy Mexico's Ministry of Tourism: cover, title page,
pages 4, 12, 18

Library of Congress Cataloging-in-Publication Data

Conlon, Laura, 1959-
    Products of Mexico / by Laura Conlon.
        p.   cm. — (South of the border)
    Includes index.
    ISBN 1-55916-053-5
    1. Mexico—Industries—Juvenile literature. 2. Agriculture—
Economic aspects—Mexico—Juvenile literature. 3. Mexico—
Manufactures—Juvenile literature. 4. Mexico—Economic
conditions—1982- —Juvenile literature. [1. Mexico.] I. Title.
II. Series.
HC123.C66   1994
338.0972—dc20
                                                    94-15907
                                                    CIP
                                                    AC
Printed in the USA

TABLE OF CONTENTS

PRODUCTS OF MEXICO

Did you know one of the most popular foods in the United States first came from Mexico? Chocolate comes from the beans of the **cacao** tree. Other food products that come from Mexico are tomatoes, vanilla and peanuts.

These are a few of the many natural resources grown on Mexican farms today. Other natural resources provide Mexican people with jobs in fishing, forestry, mining, industry and tourism.

Mexican farms produce a wide variety of vegetables and fruits

FARMING

Most of the farmland in Mexico is used to grow corn — the Mexican people's basic food. Mexico must also **import** corn from other countries to meet its needs. Cotton is the main crop farmers **export,** or send to other countries.

Most of the corn, bean and cotton farms are in central Mexico. Coffee, sugar cane, cacao — chocolate — and fruit are grown in the warmer, wetter tropical regions.

In many **remote** areas, farming is still done by hand or with oxen.

Under threat of rain, a Mexican farmer plows the earth with a team of horses

FARM ANIMALS

Land in Mexico that is not good for farming is often used for grazing. Beef cattle graze in the dry, northern land. Dairy cattle are raised in central Mexico. Goats are raised on very rugged, rocky lands. Chickens, sheep and horses are also raised in Mexico.

A vaquero, or Mexican cowboy, herds cattle on a ranch in northern Mexico

FISHING

Most Mexican fishermen work along Mexico's Pacific Coast. They catch large amounts of tuna and sardines. Fishermen catch many lobsters and snappers off the Gulf of Mexico. Shrimp is a major resource on both the Atlantic and Pacific Coasts. Most of Mexico's seafood is exported.

In remote villages, Indians use large "butterfly nets" to catch fish.

A Mexican fishing boat is anchored in the harbor at Ensenada

Many Mexicans live on what they earn from selling handmade products

*More than 4 million visitors travel to Mexico each year,
and many of them visit the Mayan ruins at Chichén Itzá*

FORESTRY

Many products come from the thick, tropical rain forests of Mexico. The lumber from mahogany, ebony and rosewood trees is used to make beautiful furniture. **Chicle** is taken from sapodilla trees. Chicle is used to make chewing gum. Ule trees produce rubber. The beans — seeds — from cacao trees make chocolate.

In the cooler regions of Mexico, people plant and cut pine trees for lumber and papermaking.

As rain forests in southern Mexico are cut down, farmers plant the open ground with food crops

OIL AND NATURAL GAS

Mexico's greatest wealth comes from oil, its top export. Mexico is the fourth largest oil-producing country in the world. More than a billion barrels of oil are produced each year. Most of the oil is drilled from undersea wells in the Gulf of Mexico.

Mexico is also one of the world's leading producers of natural gas.

This is one of several Mexican oil refineries — places where oil is processed

MINING

Long ago, tales of silver and gold lured Spanish explorers to Mexico. Today mining provides jobs for millions of Mexicans.

Mexico is the world's leading producer of silver. Mexican craftspeople use silver, which is found underground, to create beautiful jewelry and ornaments. These are mostly exported or sold to tourists.

Copper, lead, gold, iron ore and coal are also mined.

Silver products from Mexican mines glitter at a market in Taxco

TOURISM

More than 4 million tourists visit Mexico each year. Most of them are American. Tourists enjoy sunny beaches, like those at Acapulco and Cancun.

Tourists are amazed by Mexico's colorful history when they visit the ancient ruins of the Mayan and Aztec cultures.

Visitors buy beautiful handmade clothing, pottery and jewelry from Mexican craftspeople.

Tourists enjoy a dinner on a beach in Baja California, Mexico

INDUSTRY

Mexico's capital, Mexico City, is the center for **industry.** The largest industry is **textiles,** or cloth. Some textile factories weave cotton into a rough white cloth called *manta.* Mexicans use manta to make clothing of Indian designs. Other textile factories make fabrics out of wool and silk.

Another important industry is steel. Monterrey, in northern Mexico, is the major steel-producing city.

Glossary

cacao (kah KAH oh) — a tropical tree; its beans — seeds — are used to make chocolate

chicle (CHEEK lay) — sap from the sapodilla tree, which is used to make chewing gum

export (EKS port) — to sell goods to another country

import (IM port) — to buy goods from another country

industry (IN dus tree) — businesses and factories that make goods

remote (re MOTE) — far away or out-of-the-way

textile (TEKS tile) — fabric made by weaving or knitting

INDEX